NOTE TO
SELF

JERMAINE L. STEARNS

Jermaine L. Stearns, JL3Brand
Hope Mills, North Carolina
www.jl3brand.com

Note to Self/ Jermaine L. Stearns
ISBN 979-8-218-18390-

Dedicated to the inner person I want

to become!

"*SET YOURSELF FREE!!*"

-JERMAINE L. STEARNS

CONTENTS

YOU DON'T KNOW EVERYTHING

Being born a leader and being assigned a leader, could be problematic for a few who serve in this capacity. As leaders, being in the know and knowing everything are two different things. When you are in the know you're made aware, but when one knows, they are knowledgeable. It is quite impossible for one person to know everything because if you knew everything, is there room for you to know nothing in order to learn something?

A leader once said to me, "Pastor J, the person who answers the questions is the Pastor." Now while this was in reference to being a leader in ministry, it is simple but can also be complex. It's simple because it's a great thing to know material, but complex when you swear, you're a walking dictionary who has no flaws. We call this a *"know it all"* type of person. A "know-it-all," is defined as a person who acts as though he or she knows everything and dismisses the opinions or comments and suggestions of others. This makes them an easy target! Too much right? If we pay close attention to this definition, the word "acts" is key. One who appears to know it all, is merely acting as if they do but they really do not. They create their own play and star in every role, but are just good at acting like they do! It is like having a form of being knowledgeable but probably scared of the power of knowledge.

As I examined myself on this day, I found beauty in the form of not knowing. Do you realize that there is freedom in sometimes just not knowing? You can put too much pressure on yourself by trying to know everything, and really be good at nothing. The power of being free is not just in the physical, but it pays to be free mentally as well. I found that when questions were being posed to me about certain topics and since I was the one in charge or the leader, I pressured myself in trying to find the answer, but realized it took a whole lot of energy to attempt to fix or have the answer to a problem, when the truth of the matter was that I really just didn't know. I was creating a ditch with no ladder to get out of it. It was pressure trying to be a "know it all," acting on a stage with no skill. Wow, what foolery!

It's ok to know some things and to be the one to answer the questions sometimes but being seen as a "know it all" may ricochet. Be honest with yourself when being presented with a question or subject you are not knowledgeable in and just admit, I don't know! This admission saves face from your mouth writing a check your behind can't cash. Just free yourself, save your time and others' time, and be honest. You really do not know everything that you think you know. Knowledge is power, but too much power can kill you.

Note to Self: You don't know everything.

Reflection:

Reflect on a moment when you were so sure about what you knew about a particular situation and you later found out you were wrong. Write it down and express your viewpoint of yourself afterwards.

"Knowledge is power, but too much power can kill you." Jermaine L. Stearns

YOU CAN RECEIVE CONSTRUCTIVE CRITICISM… IT'S OK

In 2018 social media and technology offered us the opportunity to connect with the world around us unlike ever before. We can now have staff meetings in another country via webcam or live stream. We can also see animals give birth in another continent without ever leaving our homes. We can even allow distant relatives to connect with us via social media as if they were with us all the time. In fact, social media may be the quickest way to grow your personal business, be in tune with world news and the latest fashions. It serves a great purpose when used correctly. However, it can be a place where people may receive negative feedback about something that, in their view, is a very positive thing. Social media viewers have the capability to give opinions and criticism that for the wrong person receiving the criticism, could be their final day on planet earth.

Society, or should I say the opinions of others, has become the driving force to some people's appearance, lifestyles, and even relationship status. People's perspectives matter to them, and now their perspectives have become a motivation to please others, and not God or themselves! We have all been in a place where certain people we trust, and love have shaped some of our decisions in this walk of life. It has guided us to some great places and molded us to make some sound decisions for the advancement of goals and future opportunities. This is what I call constructive criticisms. The ability to give sound advice to assist in development, without any intent to destroy a person. The basis of this is love. Loving a person enough to give them feedback that will improve them. Now, this doesn't mean that everything that an individual is given is going to feel good. It means the person on the receiving end understands the intent and takes it as motivation. It is exactly what it is, constructive! We must learn to know the difference between when a person is trying to help versus trying to destroy. How do we look out for this? By spending time developing a relationship is one factor, but we must know their hearts and motives also.

Research shows that focusing on the situation and not the person, giving recommendations on how to improve, and not making assumptions are helpful tips in constructive criticism! It is a healthy balance and has substance that someone could grow from. As stated earlier, you must be open to the other person, and know they have your best interests at heart. In my opinion, this is a very critical place simply because the person on the receiving end cannot be defensive or guarded to receive the criticism. This is not effective for either party.

It takes a level of trust and accountability to be able to receive advice from others. It can be a hard place for some due to their past experiences with trusting others and letting their guard down. In fact, it can be downright painful, but without experiencing pain you'll never know how to receive healing!

When you allow yourself to grow in your confidence, you can receive criticism if it empowers and pushes you to go to the next level as a conqueror! As I stated on social media, everyone is not out to harm you. Some people are meant to be your pusher, not your destroyer! It is ok to receive criticism as long as it's constructive. Grow from love!

1.   If you could finish this statement, how would you? I am the most critical of how I...

2.   We are often our worst critic. Why are you your worst critic?

3.   Who is that one person at the top of your list you can receive constructive criticism from and why is that person the one?

YOU DO NOT HAVE TO ALWAYS VOICE YOUR OPINION

Have you ever heard your parent(s) or friends say you just talk too much? Most of the time when this statement was made to you, it wasn't because you said something flattering. It was most likely because you said something that should have not been said, whether it was at the wrong time, or to the wrong person, or just said for no reason. For me it was always from my mother! It was always something that she said that I overheard (being nosey) or I was the one she spoke to that I apparently was to keep to myself, but at the wrong time I unleashed the dragon and it was all she wrote. I let whatever it was lose. Not only did I spill the beans, I gave my extra two cents about the matter that nine times out of 10 had nothing to do with me! I was just voicing my opinion!

The Freedom of Speech amendment is something that we as citizens use so much until they need to create another amendment to fix this one.

Learning to keep your mouth close is a good behavior trait to possess. In other words, it is ok to just Shut-Up. Now, I am not saying having an opinion isn't good. I am simply stating that being too opinionated can hurt you, and the truth of the matter is that not everyone wants to hear it. I have come to realize that there is a time and place to be vocal and exercising wisdom is key. Think of the times you opened your mouth pertaining to a matter that had nothing to do with you and you received a response such as, "mind your own business," this has nothing to do with you!". Think about how this made you feel. If you're like me, instead of backing down you got defensive, and your defense caused you to take it personal, and your personal feelings caused you to buck up. Wait, but truthfully, IT REALLY HAD NOTHING TO DO WITH YOU! What occurred is that you placed a judgment about something that wasn't actually based on facts or knowledge about a matter. You invited yourself to the party! Just showed up unannounced, and no one likes a party crasher.

Let's look at another scenario. Have you ever been asked your opinion and you still got lashed on because the person that requested your viewpoint didn't like what you said? Sometimes it just seems that whatever you say will cause a backlash and just will not be received. There is no solution for this, it is just life.

Forming your opinion is not wrong, but giving it when it is not solicited may not be the best, and giving it when it is requested can still be a problem. Use wisdom in all situations and just shut up when warranted. Your opinion matters, just not to everyone.

Recall two moments, if any, when you were told to mind your business and express how that phrase made you feel.

1.

2.

YOUR NOSE IS NOT AS BIG AS YOU THINK IT IS! MIND YOUR OWN BUSINESS

Question of the day, can you really see the tip of your nose? Really? Can you see it without looking in the mirror? If the answer to this question is no, that's how much WE should mind our own business.

Being a pastor of a ministry and an outgoing guy, I like to pride myself on minding my own business. But honestly, it is a tough thing to do, when you want to be in the loop of everything, and even the loop goes into circles.

I can recall going through my mom's senior yearbook and she had nosy written either beside a girl's name or on the picture of her face, in the book. Either way she was deemed to be nosy in my mom's sight. I wonder why that was exactly? There it goes again.

In my research and experience with myself and others, I have come to find that being nosy has its positive and negative associations. Most individuals who are nosy, are often obsessed with other people's affairs, and could possibly compare the news to their own personal life. This in fact could be food for the nosy one to give them insight of how well they are doing with their own life. They may also want to see if their life measures up to the person they are "spying" on or if their life is better than theirs. This could be a positive outlook in the form of one looking to grow, however, mostly like to none, the basis of this premise is to just be nosy! In fact, being nosy leaves room for one to go and spread rumors, which could be catastrophic, especially if their motives are impure.

PRIDE CAN LEAVE YOU DAMAGED AND CAUSE YOU TO MISS OUT

2016 was a challenging year for me and my family. We left a ministry that we were a part of for over 8 years, we had a family of 3 living with us, and I was without a job. Financial difficulties seemed to have hit my house and beyond that death also stopped by to visit us.

A few Christmases back my family and I visited Columbia, South Carolina where my wife and I are originally from. We normally don't get a chance to visit there much, but when we do; we do. Upon our visit we stopped to see a few family members, one included my oldest brother and his then wife. Our visit was very pleasant, but unfortunately without seeing my brother. Leaving without the interaction of my brother, left me a little concerned, but also bothered due to his level of response that I later found out served a purpose. Once we left Columbia that evening, it would be a year before I saw him again, let alone speak to him, and by the time I saw him, he was lifeless. My oldest brother was deceased and I did not speak to him one last time.

That moment in his wife's salon left me speechless and bitter! I walked away bothered that my own brother, the eldest of three, didn't want to see me or my family. For a whole year I refused to call him. You see, from my perspective, I figured the phone worked two ways. He had my number like I had his, and that if he wanted to see or speak to us, since he dismissed us last time, it was his responsibility to make it happen. But was it? For the year that I didn't speak to my brother, I later learned that he had been dealing with a lot. He was dealing with health issues, being a husband, father, and a provider. All of which is enough to deal with his own demons.

As stated before, that summer was a beast with all we were dealing with and to add fuel to the fire, we were also without communication via phone and or internet. By being disconnected from the outside world, the only way we could keep in touch was at our job source. I remember that Wednesday morning like it was yesterday. The night before, I had just encouraged my family that we have been through a lot that summer and things could have been a lot worse. I refused to mention what the worst could have been in order to not deal with it, but unspoken, I was referring to death. So, When I walked into the workplace and connected my disconnected phone to the internet via Wi-Fi, almost immediately my phone began to chime and scream for attention. I saw several missed messenger calls from a cousin and when I was able to, I made contact. I heard wailing and crying in the background, and my first line of response was, "what's wrong?" The reply I heard sent chills up my spine, my voice left my soundbox and my feet became numb. My oldest brother is dead! Found lying lifeless and never to return. He left before a goodbye or an I love you could be said or heard. To be more transparent, he left without a word from me within a year. He died and I was full of pride!

In the following days, not only did I have to come to grips that he was gone, but I had to bring myself to be able to comfort his wife, children, family, and confidants. I was left with the honor and task to say my final goodbyes without a return response from the one who I looked up too. The days, weeks, months, and year following his death were rough, in fact just this past year I started to mourn and face the demon of pride. Reflecting over this moment I realized that as I was eulogizing him, it was like death speaking over death. What does that mean? Pride caused me to miss out on life because it killed the part of me from living-to being life for my brother. God began to deal with me, that due to pride I missed out on the opportunities to show his love. Pride made me forget that I was an ambassador for Christ and that the love God had shown me, I was supposed to be the bigger example in the matter with my brother Marion. I was supposed to be the mature one.

Even though Marion was the oldest of us, I was the "mature one" in Christ. But even though I was the "mature one" I had a lot of growing up to do! You see, we are not exempt from falling or making a mistake, it is just a reminder that we are all on this journey to become better or at least we should be. The death of Marion "Pooh" was just not about him, but about a part of me that had to die as well. God works in mysterious ways, right? So mysterious that he would use death as a teaching tool to save you. Pride is a stronghold but not so strong that God can't handle him. Remember life is too precious, don't let something that isn't bigger than God, cause you to miss out on living!

Note to self: Pride Reflection

1.On a scale to 1 t0 5 how would you rate pride working in your life?

Circle: 1   2   3   4   5
1 being the lowest and 5 being the highest

2. List 3 areas that you feel you are prideful in and or that may have or will cause you to miss out on something.

1. _____
2. _____
3. _____

"The best way to get rid of Pride is to be truthful about you!"

~Jermaine Stearns

GET OVER THE ME SYNDROME

Me Me ME, I.... I.... I.... is a problem that a lot of us have that we don't even know about! Being certain again and behaving younger than the age you are can be   problematic. I have seen grown men and women often revert to childish ways simply because what is transpiring in their life is a result of them being selfish and self-centered. When a person is always self-centered, careless of others thoughts and feelings, and behaves in this manner, I call this the ME SYNDROME. Everything is centered around them and only them. Have you ever behaved this way, or have been in a company who exemplifies this kind of characteristics?

I have not only witnessed this through the lens of other people, but I have also experienced it by looking in the mirror at myself. Wanting things my way, not concerned about who it affects, as long as I got what I wanted. Just unruly and ugly! Our behavior does not only affect our future, but it affects the now as well as how people can and will view us. Selfness is a disease that can ruin a nation if we are not careful.

The bible speaks about men becoming lovers of themselves, **2 Timothy 3:2**. People who deal with loving themselves only, having a desire for worldly positions, being abusive and being utterly ungrateful and so much. These are more systems of the desire that we must be careful of in our walk of life, especially for us as a born-again believer.

How do we overcome the ME SYNDROME? By exchanging your will for the will of the father. See this syndrome isn't about material things, but it all boils down to the matter of your heart! Are you willing to submit your desire for his desire? Your plans for his plans? Your thoughts for his thoughts? Even your attitude for his attitude towards things. Overcoming it is simple. Just simply allow yourself to be submitted to selfless acts of love and most importantly to the will of our father.

Today ask yourself, has my life been all about me and what I got and what I can achieve? Or even ask yourself, how can today not be about me but about what God wants for me today?

There is nothing wrong with accomplishments and obtaining things, but if Christ is left out of the equation, then everything else is worthless. Remember our life isn't happening to us, it is happening for us to be an example for someone else to grow. Me Syndrome can be a beast! Are you the beast of your life?

FRUSTRATION CAN KILL YOU

Have you ever tried and tried and tried and it just seemed like you were getting NOWHERE? It seems like every effort was in vain? It appeared that if annoyed was a person he would be your best friend?

I think we have all been in this place for sure at least once in our lifetime. For some of us, it seems like we live on the street of frustration, especially when you know you have the ability to accomplish a thing or feel things should work out just because.

Frustration comes from the fact that we do not have the ability to change or achieve something that we desire. WHERE DID THIS MONSTER COME FROM? Most of the time it comes from the mere fact that we want to be in control and the reality is we can't. Control is a method that has been developed due to an experience where either you have been stripped of a right and felt violated or that one isn't use to submitting to authority. I took a deep look at my own life and saw how not being in control of some things made me feel. I realized it was due to me not wanting to submit to what was out of my hands and in the hands of the heavenly father. The concern I had with trusting the father was not that he couldn't handle the situation, but the concern was me letting go!

The hardest thing to do sometimes is letting go of what you have been handling for so long. The moment we are asked to release it, the frustration often builds and could cause us to kill the possibility of the "trust factor" in God. The very system that God uses to establish relationship; is also known as FAITH.

Frustration could be a monster to your faith walk if you let it. However, if you reverse that idea, it literally could be the thing that promotes you to the next phase or level of your life. How is that? Oftentimes the very thing that we don't have control over and are irritated about, is the very thing that God wants to use to free us and allow us to step on top of it to reach your mountain peak.

Your possibility to be the next best, or become the greatest, or accomplish what seems to be accomplishable, can be destroyed by staying stuck in anger or by being annoyed all the time. Don't allow how you feel to determine your destination, for God isn't moved by your feelings, he is moved by your determination to conquer and defeat in what seems to be frustrating you.

Today I encourage you to look at frustration as your step stool and rise above the issues to cut off its head. Release the control and watch God move in your day!

"Frustration doesn't change things, it hinders them!"~Jermaine Stearns

NOT THE PLAN OF GOD

"Then Jesus said, "Come to me, all of you who are weary and carry heavy burdens, and I will give you rest."
Matthew 11: 28

Today is not the day to be heavy; you have too much life, work, and assignments to complete. Today is the day of confession!

Today I am not overwhelmed. Today I am free from past hurts, sins, frustration, and distress. Today is my day of freedom from being burdened down and pressed to no degree. Today is my moment of victory and being triumphant in my endeavors.

I will release the things I am carrying that are too much for me. I will not give them to others, but I will cast them on the ONLY ONE who can handle them all! Today I give my overwhelmed thoughts, relationships, jobs, encounters and desires to you Father. Today is my day of confession and change.

I decree that I am not overwhelmed. I will not be like a ship toast by the winds on the sea. I am on stable ground which is the word of God. I am whole in my process and today I stand up right with my heart lifted before the father and any oppression on my life, hanging above my head is in your hands father. For today I surrender being overwhelmed, in Jesus' name, AMEN!

Today I released being overwhelmed in

_____

_____

_____

_____

_____

_____

Today I will not pick it back up because

_____

_____

_____

_____

_____

_____

CONQUER THIS CYCLE

Cycle(s) is defined as, "a series of events that are regularly repeated in the same order."

The first thing I think about when I hear the word CYCLE is a bicycle. I imagine the wheels going in the same direction at the same speed. Isn't it interesting the way this inventor created a moving invention that would go in the same direction at the same time but not without a driving force to propel it forward? That is how bicycles work! Someone must produce the power to make it move forward. As we parallel that to our personal, unspoken cycle(s), aren't we the driving force behind why we keep doing the same thing? Going to the same places? Behaving the same way?

Cycles to me is repetitive behavior ~~that is~~ entangled with the lack of discipline and control.

We often repeat what we have not conquered! Not conquering a thing may result in a bad pattern of behavior that we enjoy in the flesh, which results from a lack of being disciplined enough to stop the cycle. The rotating of the wheels on the bike are designed to do that! That is what they were designed for, but you were not created to repeat behaviors that are setup to keep you from migrating to the next phase of your life.

Why do we continue the cycle? We could possibly not know who we are and what we were designed to conquer. Maybe we like what we do too much to let go! You do not have to continue in a pattern that you were not designed to participate in. Today you can choose to stop or to keep on spinning! You have those options but remember you were created as a conquer. Be the driving force in your life, not repeating things that are driving you!

"Your consistent path around the mountain may create your avalanche of destruction!"

~Jermaine Stearns

JUMP FORWARD

Waking up each morning to matters you have been holding on to can affect your future and how you see it.

Do you realize that when you peek through the scoop of your eyes each day you wake up to your future? Most of the time we just see it as a day to continue the cycles of work tasks, family tasks, or just overall a new day. While that may be a fact, your outlook on how you feel could possibly change, from it just being a day versus waking up to your future.

The question often isn't what you are holding on to, it should be why are you holding on to it? Understanding your why is important to solving and understanding some of the very issues we often hold on to. What is your reason for holding on or for not letting go?

When I was a kid, we would go swimming almost every day during the summer months at a place called *Trenum Park*. My cousins and I would jump straight into the pool after we got in our swimming trunks and showered. They used to jump into the deep end while some jumped off the diving board and little me would jump in an area where my feet would touch the bottom. It was my safe place!

One day I had enough of being left alone in the shallows. I wanted to experience something new and different, but mostly I was tired of being left behind. So, I made up my mind that I was going to leave this place of shallows, I was going to swim with the big boys. Before going to the next level, I had to take a test. I had to pass the level I was on to prove that I could handle what was on the other end of the rope. The problem with this is that I had seen many swimmers fail at trying to swim from one end of the pool to the other end without stopping. Recalling their attempts would have discouraged anyone but I wasn't going to let their failures stop my victory. After getting the rope I made my way to the other end and back without stopping and I passed the test. I was free to join the band, run with the horse, simply swim with the big boys. I had arrived, so I thought!

After getting to the other side of the pool, there was no turning back for me! "I had come too far to turn back now," as the mature saints would say. Everything I had known by swimming in the shallows suddenly changed. There was no more bottom for my feet to touch and there were not as many people as before. I had stepped into an area that required more of me. I was now required to tread water and use more muscles. I even had to build up my level of holding my breath sometimes until I reached the edge of the pool to gather myself. I was in a different world even though it was the same pool I had seen all my life. The fact that I was in a BIG POOL now was the ultimate test to my new level, to not only see if I could swim, but a test of my bravery. I had to jump off the diving board! You think the test of swimming back and forth was the beast, the mere fact that this board was high and suspended about 12 feet above water caused the 98-pound little boy to shiver. I had seen many people, including my cousin, jump off this board but seeing and actually doing it are two different things! One day my cousins finally talked me into trying it. They persuaded me to go to the other side of the rope and this time wasn't any different. They wanted me to experience the joy and excitement that they would have Saturday after Saturday, but I later realized they wanted me to accomplish a level of fear. So, after much talk and conversations I finally got the nerve to do it. I was going to jump off the diving board but first had to climb up a ladder to get to the board. Reaching the top, felt like making it to the rails of destiny. It felt like the bottom of my stomach was going to fall out of my body and that all the water I had dripping from me was drying up really fast. The noise of kids splashing in the water below, simply became a background to my event. I was at the top looking down the mouth of the pool. It was now or never! After standing there for a moment, it hit me that I only had two options: Jump or turn back! The problem with turning back was that I had to not only face the people who were waiting to jump at the bottom of the ladder, but I had to hear about how scared I was for not wanting to jump. I had to FACE ME! I had to face the very person I was trying to let go of, the person fearful of holding onto not letting go. After a few more thoughts and looking down a few more times, I found myself in the middle of the pool, swimming back to the edge! I made it! I did it! But how? Sitting back and reflecting on the how, I discovered what it was that caused me to jump. It was beyond facing the fear, it was the letting go part. I had simply just let go and moved forward. I had to go against all of whatever I was holding on to in order to accomplish all that was in front of me. While this took some time for me to accomplish, it did not mean that it couldn't have done it sooner. The only thing stopping me from letting go was me. As you reflect on what it is that you are holding on to today, ask yourself, why? What is the purpose of holding on to this? Once you come to those answers the next thing to do is, let go, move forward, and jump into your next level. Today might just be your day!

Reflection:

What am I holding on to that I need to let go?

_____

_____

_____

_____

Why am I holding on to it?

_____

_____

_____

_____

_____

PERFECT PEOPLE DON'T EXIST

Living in a world of social media where everything seems to be timeless and often presented as perfect is a concern for the future of living. Our lives are slowly being shaped and molded into an image that isn't realistic. Our kids are merely taking their own lives not because of not having friends, but merely because their life isn't what they want it or think it should be. Now, that is not necessarily the truth for all circumstances and situations, but it has played a starring role in the life of many.

Speaking with many individuals during the pastoral assignment and even battling with it myself, I have often seen people struggle with their truth and reality of where they have come from. These people have gotten so accustomed to living a certain lifestyle that they seem to have grown beyond a point of self-reflection and have developed an idea that they have never had an issue, fault, or struggle! That where they are now, is where they have always been. No shameful experience, no lack of rejection and no sense of ever having hopelessness, let alone no voice to a testimony.

It's amazing living in a society where this exists let alone in the house of prayer (church). Many people in the 21st century do not attend church not because of the way one worships or the style or method of delivering a message, but simply because of the lack of truth from a person. Many of these truth liars often paint the picture that their lives are full of perfection, that their breath doesn't stink, and that they live above fault. These methods and ideologies are often the hindrance to the growth and the relatability to helping other people overcome. They clearly are not relatable. You see the Word of God tells us that we are overcomers by the blood of the lamb and by the word of our testimony. You can't have a testimony by being perfect! It is the imperfection that you have overcome that causes other people to believe that they can too. It is called being down to earth.

I can recall a time when I tried to encourage and warn someone about a situation and they told me that they were spiritual enough to see if there was something wrong. This situation devastated me for several reasons. One, I didn't want my friend to end up in a situation that I could have possibly saved them from, secondly, I wanted my own experience to help them! Instead of being received, I was rejected, and silenced as a friend even though I was crying aloud. I was made to feel that I didn't fit on their level and that they were perfect. This situation never stopped me from loving them or wanting the best for them. The situation made me realize that they were not in a place to receive or even be free. You see we all have not arrived. Someone else that could merely be saved because of what you have overcome.

Having your nose so far in the air that you can't smell the flowers on the ground will cause people to never experience a level of overcoming because of one not being relatable. There are no perfect people! All of us have a story to tell! It is the telling part that helps us all reach perfection(maturity).

If I could in courage you today, remember you have a story to tell and everything you see is not gold, it's just glittery to paint a picture of perfection! Do not be fooled today! See them beyond what they post and how they behave. See them for who they really are and remember you might have something in common.

POTENTIAL

What behavior(s) do you possess that are hindering you from your potential?

Today I renounce the behavior and the patterns of...
(finish the sentence)

TODAY I AM FEELING

Often, we do not give ourselves permission to feel. Today I want you to take a moment and reflect on how you are feeling. A wise woman, who I trust, said to me, "IT'S OK TO NOT BE OK!" ~Veronica Kelly.

So, in this moment, reflect on yourself and be honest by finishing this statement.

TODAY I AM FEELING:

MOVE ON

A few years ago, I was sitting with my best friend of over 27 years, and somehow, we got into a conversation about me graduating from college. As the conversation progressed, I had an Aha moment. You know, that moment when you get a revelation about something you had no clue about? Yes, that moment! Aha had found me and I wasn't ready to deal with him at the restaurant.

When an aha moment kicked in, I suddenly realized I had been stuck in this place for 8 years all because of death. The death of my mother! I realized that I didn't want to move forward with the accomplishment of obtaining a degree because my pusher was no longer with me. It seemed that me being an achiever was also me abandoning or moving on without her, and I refused to do so.

Fast forwarding 2 years later, my oldest brother passed away and I had to relive the moment all over again. My brother and mother were 10 years apart in age, my brother and I were 10 years apart in age, and his son and I are 10 years apart in age. When I began to reflect on this, I once again became stuck in the thought of will I ever be successful before leaving this world? To try and face the mud that had me bound and to keep the legacy of my mother alive, I set a goal of writing a cookbook in her honor. Everything I needed for the book was right inside of me, and I finished it with blood, sweat and tears. It was edited, and the book cover looked great, it was finished! But was it? Was there something missing in it? One more recipe? Let's change the picture on the cover, I began to think. None of that made sense, it was complete, but I wasn't. I was not ready to deal with the unknown.

"Jay, what's going on with the book?" Is what they would ask! "Umm. it's finished, I just need…, well, its umm..," is what I begin to say, not grasping I was addicted to excuses. Excuses were the driving force of me being afraid of accomplishments. You see, anything centered around me reaching a goal and being successful, I had a problem with and I started making excuses as to why I could not succeed. Yes, SUCCESS was my issue and yet making excuses was the root. Talking with my wife one day, as tears fell from my eyes, I got the revelation that I did not want to accomplish anything without my mother. That was the moment I exposed the root of the excuse for who he was! Not wanting to be in the pity party with him any longer, I made a conscious decision I was going to come out and being stuck was no longer an option!

After speaking with my wife, and my dear sister Veronica, I realized I had to give myself permission to move on! Accepting that me moving on had nothing to do with forgetting my mother and her legacy was difficult but knowing that if she was here, she would want me to be successful, began to give me peace. So, I did it, I gave myself permission! I started the process of digging myself out, while crying and hurting- I was determined, I wanted to be free! I graduated from Andersonville Theological Seminary, finished my first book, *Food for Thought*, and now working on picking up the pieces of where my life stopped 10 years ago, I made a choice! I choose to deal with excuses and give him his eviction notice, and I choose to be free!

Being free is an option! Either you want it or you don't. Sometimes life brings us circumstances and situations that could have us stuck and we do not even know it. But it is only when you allow yourself to be open and deal with yourself that one can realize just how stuck they are.

I encourage you to look at yourself and ask yourself, what is keeping me from moving forward? Or what fears do I have that are causing me to not be successful or accomplished? Once you have found the answers, deal with it and give yourself your permission to move forward to your next promise!!

Note to self, Permission to move forward, reflection:

What are some areas of your life you need to give yourself permission to move forward in?

1. _____
2. _____
3. _____

Philippians 3: 13-14

13 Brethren, I count not myself to have apprehended: but this one thing I do, forgetting those things which are behind, and reaching forth unto those things which are before, 14 I press toward the mark for the prize of the high calling of God in Christ Jesus.

BACK OFF

Jermaine, back off! Trying to fit a square into a circle is not going to work. In the end you may injure the square and the circle, trying to make something work that just doesn't!

Have you ever tried to fix something and during the process of trying to make it right, you were doing more damage than you realize? After you gathered that you were not the one for the job, did you call someone in to fix the problem who was actually qualified to do so? Ok, let's be honest, maybe not that exact example but something similar?

Either way, there have been some things in our life that we thought we could handle but are just not equipped to. That was me, a person that thought he could fix everything, especially people. I am a good person, a minister, wait I'm a Pastor, I was born for this, I got this, "I told myself." Well, not so! In life, there are lessons that will come and teach you a few things about people and your capabilities. People, their behavior and perspective are not areas that we as believers should try to change, that's a job for the one who created them.

In my short time of being on this earth and having a desire to help, I have come to learn that the best way to help is backing off! Backing off isn't always a bad thing to do. The results of keeping your distance can leave room for a lot of things to take place in one's life, such as healing, forgiveness and even a time of self-reflection. This gives time for you and others to look at themselves and circumstances in a different light. Trying to force things that one may not be ready to receive or adjust too, will actually or could hurt the person more. It could box a person into a corner, where walls were on the brink to come down, but due to a lack of discernment and observation, you became the person to add fuel to a fire causing a massive explosion that could backfire and kill you.

Helping others is a selfless act and requires time and energy. If one is not careful on how to aid in helping, they can become damaged in the process. I am merely saying backing off gives one time to refresh and to explore other options about them and others. Remember you are a person as well, not helping in some forms is considered helping. It is ok to just back off.

Note to self, back off Moment:

Who do you need to back off from, and why?

1.　　I need to back off from _____
because I _____

_____.

2.　I　also　need　to　back　off　from
_____, because I realize
that _____.

　　Maybe you don't need to back away from someone, maybe it's something. List a few things you know you need to back away from or back off from, because it is doing more harm than good.

　　I need to back off or away from the following things:

　　1.　_____
　　2.　_____
　　3.　_____

"This above all: to thine own self be true!" ~Sir William Shakespeare

CONFIDENCE LIES IN YOUR PURPOSE

On this journey to rediscover who I was intended to be, from the foundations of me knowing my existence, has been a task. I found myself one on one dealing with things that I thought that I had already conquered. In fact, things that I was re-facing caused me to reflect that I wasn't as perfect as I thought I was. The ugly truth of what had been lying within was now confronting my confidence in who I thought I was. There was a war going on between confidence and low self-esteem, and while they were at battle, the war would soon confront and perfect who I needed to be.

Coming up as the only child of my father and mother, not expecting to be in this world, it seemed as if the odds were already stacked against me! Having to deal with the unknown of two worlds colliding before my existence and development, the creator still had a plan to remind me of who I was! Just within the last year I was told that I was just as good as everyone. What People failed to see was that they had experienced my work as a photographer, a friend, and a pastor, but didn't know that while they saw my purpose, I lacked the confidence in my purpose.

Confidence isn't something that you get at the local food mart, or the nearest gas station, it is something drenched into you before the foundations of your name were verbalized in the earth by your guardians. It is something that is embedded into your DNA but nurtured by those around you who possess the ability to cultivate what's in you. Your confidence does not have anything to do with how you look, dress, or even speak. But Confidence really has to do with how much you love and value yourself. When we can get to the point of loving and valuing ourselves enough how God does with careful nurturing by the right hands, confidence will begin to shine just like the sun leaping off of earth.

Before confidence can be exemplified, I am a firm believer we must get to know who we are or were intended to be. You see, we must learn about ourselves before anyone else does. Knowing what we have been chosen to do beyond the camera, careers, children, and spouses gives us the ability to deal with confidence in our purpose. Once we have mastered who we are and whose we are, the purpose of what we are to accomplish can be rendered with confidence in knowing we have been chosen to do a thing. Remember, you have a purpose, but your purpose cannot be completely fulfilled unless you understand the confidence that you need is right within knowing your purpose.

Name a few areas that you feel you may be lacking confidence in?

1._____

2._____

3._____

Once you have completed the above area, think of 3 goals that you can embark on to achieve confidence in the following areas.

1. I WILL achieve confidence in the 1st area by

2. I WILL overcome the lack of confidence in area 2 by

3. My confidence level in area 3 is lacking because of

ALLOW GOD TO RESCUE YOU FROM YOURSELF

There was a sermon series that I ministered, entitled *The Deliverance Cycle*. God instructed me that the process of deliverance is a continuous process, and produces lessons of going in and out of the issues of life. Upon my research the definition of deliverance is, the process of being rescued or set free. Defining the word deliverance by google search, gave me new insight of what deliverance really meant. As I studied the word rescue, I understood that there were some things that myself and others needed to be rescued from.

Many movie writers have told the story lines of individuals having a great time with friends on ships and plans, headed to a destination filled with fun and laughter, and within minutes, all their joy seems to be washed away by a storm causing their lives to be shipwrecked with no help in sight. Some may have found themselves on remnants of the mode of transportation, others may have been submerged in water with no way of escaping the blue sea that holds them in the hollow of its hand. Their lives seem to have no more purpose. Living but seemingly lifeless.

After recalling some of these films, such as *The Blue Lagoon*, Castaway, *Titanic* and even the sitcom, *Gilligan's Island*, I found that these films all experienced wreckage, either by storm or by human error. While pondering on whatever way the wreckage took place, I could only think of what would have been my response to a passing ship that was in sight to potentially rescue me. I gathered that I would start yelling, screaming, and even splash water to provoke the possibility of individuals seizing me from the grip of the sea. I am pretty sure I would do all that I could to be saved. Knowing how vocal I am about little matters, I understood that I would not be quiet in efforts to be rescued, that keeping my lips sealed and my voice muted would not get me to their place of freedom.

Often the pressures of life, relationships, parenting, and even cycles could appear to have us treading in water that will seemingly take us under, if we don't get out somehow. The desperation of what we are in speaks so loudly that even our silent screams have a voice. The key nugget here is that it "appears" that we will drown and the ship used to carry us to the next destination, has now become the very death of us. Maybe what appears to have left us for dead, or has caused us to be shipped wreck, is really the catalyst that postures us to be rescued.

Have you ever screamed so loud that the person closest to you still didn't hear you? Have you ever screamed so loud that you felt like you destroyed your vocal cords? By trying to reach for help, it seemed like the galaxy was blocking your voice from your silent scream being heard? This can be very uncomfortable.

We do not like to be uncomfortable! We are so accustomed to things going our way, that when we are uncomfortable, we throw tantrums like a little kid that dropped their sucker in the sand, not realizing that sometimes we are the reason why it falls in the first place. Unfamiliar with knowing that everything happens for a reason, even if it is our fault, God somehow finds a way to rescue us from whatever has occurred in our lives. Rescuing us from others isn't the main reason but for saving us from ourselves. Exam yourself, ask yourself, what is that I need to be rescued from? myself? Not everything in our lives is caused by others or about someone else! In order to be rescued from yourself you must know YOU. The process of this is not easy but it is worth knowing that whatever you stand in need of, God himself is a present help. Be reminded, it is ok to be out there on the sea, but it leaves room to be rescued, from your surroundings and even from yourself.

Note to Self, Rescue Reflection:

1.   What is your definition of Rescue?

2.   Once you have developed your own definition, now process the areas you need to be rescued in? Reach deeper and examine what you need to be rescued from within yourself.

CHECK BACK IN

For several years I have had the privilege of working for Cumberland County Schools, and wore several different hats, as a teacher assistant, computer lab director, and a bus driver to name a few. It was my last year surviving as a teacher, that somewhere in the process of wearing all those hats, I lost myself.

Have you ever booked a reservation for a hotel online? It is a simple process to reserve. All you need is a location, date, and time, along with your personal information on who the reservation is for. After you have completed this dainty task, you will receive a confirmation of your check-In process. With this confirmation a time to check into your reservation will be given. After all is paid for and confirmed, you are now on your way. Upon your arrival to the hotel destination, you present the confirmation number to the clerk, receive your room key, and you are happily checked in to where you reserved. Now, the purpose of you checking in is to temporarily house you for a set period. You never check-in anticipating having to check out early. I mean, who would want to check out of a place that they purposely wanted to be at? You purposed to check in, so you purposely want to fulfill the reservation.

I just went through this very thing! Well, not at an actual hotel but mentally and physically checked out of a place that I knew I was purposed to be. In 2017 I was called to be a teacher at an elementary school, as the third leg of the 4th grade team. I knew I was supposed to be there, the heavens spoke and everything was lined up for me to sit in this position. In fact, they called me to be on this team, and not being completely certified, but with efforts to obtain the certification. I am working 5 days a week, staying beyond the normal requirements, because I was called to this place, I had purpose in this assignment, and because it was reserved for me, I was ALL IN! I was going to be the best teacher, not just that but the best male teacher that ever-stepped foot in this school. Students were going to leave saying, Mr. Stearns is the best teacher ever, and he made a difference in my life. They were going to tell everyone about Mr. Stearns! And in all that, I was ok with checking into my reservation, I loved staying in this place. But no one prepared me for an early check out!

The semester rolls on and the parents are calling and messaging me about how their students loved me and they have seen a major improvement in their students since I was there. It went as far as a rumor started that I was getting fired. Students went home crying; some even went to get their big brothers to jump a young boy who thought he was the reason I was going to "lose" my job. But what they didn't know was that I did! Six months into the job, I was informed that there was a budget cut and I would not be able to return to the position as a 4th grade teacher. What a blow! I thought I was cool because I was kind of prepared, so I thought, but the next few days proved something different.

As the weeks went by, I started to realize that I would be on my phone more than normal during class period. That I would have spaced out moments when students would pose questions about assignments. I even became rough and insensitive to the students who I assisted in making sure they had their assignments. I started not to care! I was acting unbothered but wanted a paycheck! A colleague of mine, who knew what took place, encouraged me to hang in there. It was in that meeting with her and my team that I silently realized; I had CHECKED OUT! I had canceled my career reservations but still was living in the room. I checked out of a place where I knew I still had purpose, but was so blinded by the shift that I missed the movement.

After being encouraged by JC, who was back from maternity leave, I was walking back to my classroom and I heard a voice say, "you *have not finished the assignment, Jermaine, Check back in!*" It was at that moment that I realized that even though it looked like I was out for the count, I was reminded that the finish is just as important as the start. There was a reward and a blessing tied to me not giving up! And even though it was a challenge receiving the news about my duration ending, I still needed to complete my reservation! You see many are ok with the blessing, but not ok with what may come along with the blessings. I had to remind myself why I was there, and what my purpose was for being there. In this walk you and I will be placed with great opportunities that could change not only your life, but the life of someone else. Checking out before time means that one will quit the task given to finish. Not just finishing but finishing strong. Anytime we are appointed and assigned to do something there is a reason for interruptions that may come in the middle of the assignment.

At VCDC, I taught that there is a difference between positions and assignments! Positions are about you, but assignments are about God and his purpose! Maybe like me you have been or are being challenged in finishing an assignment that in the beginning you were 100% all in. Now you are being challenged in completing the task stronger even with obstacles right in front of you. Do not become so blinded by the obstacle that you forget to see the purpose of why you're in what you have been assigned to do. Take a moment to reflect on what, and why you are where God has called you to. Wipe the tears, brush off the heaviness and see the obstacle that has been designed for you to beat. And once you start recognizing the why, I encourage you to CHECK BACK IN. You will find in the end, that there is a greater reward in finishing then there is in quitting! If you quit, you may miss out on what you could become, but finishing proves you are what he already called you to be - more than a conquer.

RECEIVE THE PAT ON THE BACK

The saying, "small things can go a long way," has been a statement that recently I have started to watch out for. It has caused me to be more appreciative of the little things individuals do for others as well as for me. Some say that I like things big and over the top, when it comes down to being celebrated or recognized. That may be true, but I'm learning the smaller things make the loudest noise. Things that many tend to overlook such as the napkins on the dinner table, the candle on the shelf to bring light to a dark room, or even a pat on the back. These are small yet largely effective things. These small items or gestures can cause a person to be lifted and encouraged to keep going.

A teacher at the elementary school I taught at, did a small thing that became a large encouragement gesture for me to keep going that day. Every Friday, our principal developed, "the hallway huddle" where we get together in the freshness of the morning and discuss topics that would enlighten us and encourage us as educators to become better at our craft. She also designed a segment in the sessions called, celebrations.

This is where the staff had the opportunity to celebrate others or things in their personal life. I found this to be so refreshing as a staff member and looked forward to celebrating with the team and even on occasions being celebrated.

This particular day I was feeling a little low. This was during the time I was battling pride. I was discovering some of my own personal demons and how much of myself had seemed to slip away due to tragedies that caused me to miss out on life. Yea, those things! So, on this day, I decided to share a celebration, in fact it was about this book. As I was sharing the testimony about how I have felt so alone in a room full of people, and how I had some challenging moments in my classroom and such. As I was sharing, the teacher patted me on the back! And it was at that moment, it seemed I got a second wind to get up and keep going, but the challenging part of this was that I had to receive her unspoken gesture. You know how we can get sometimes, when we are down and really wanting to stay down because for some reason, we like that place? Or, we just want to be stuck where we are? That moment, I had to relinquish all that and receive her touch of reassurance, and cheer.

She had no idea that the touch made a difference, and as I reflected on the gesture, I realized it was ok to receive the pat on the back. You see, people do not have to be in your inner circle to encourage you. In fact, it is the least of them that can make the BIG difference, but the key is that you have to be open to receive what could cause you to get up from your low place. Just the simple and small things could really change your life. She had no idea of the difference or impact she had on me on that day. Just by her being moved to silently encourage me and me being open to receive caused my whole life to be changed. As I was encouraged that day, allow me to encourage you. There are going to be times where you feel like you are not worthy of the encouragement, let alone anything, but don't count yourself out. There will be individuals sent on your path who are designated to lift you up in the smallest and simplest ways, and the only thing you must do is receive it. Though the gesture may be small but yet it will be life changing to the soul.

Note to Self, Rescue Reflection:

1.   What have you consumed too much of, that made you feel overweight in life?

Have you learned from the situation?
                    YES or NO (Circle One)

                        Why or Why Not?

DON'T ABANDON POSSIBILITY

Abandonment is a serious plague in the 21st Century, in fact, it has always been an alarming issue, not just within the United States of America, but across the world. If we narrow that down within the local worship assembly there are many individuals that I have had the occasion to minister to, including myself have in some form or fashion suffered from abandonment. Most of them sit and suffer in silence, which in turn moves it to being a silent killer. I have witnessed it for myself, amongst many who are in leadership within the local worship assembly and in our community. They serve in leadership assignments such as, Pastors, Deacons, Youth Leaders, Mentors, Social Workers, Principals and Politicians. Many are afraid to address the "silent killer" and due to this, they tend to soothe their feelings by covering it up in the area of serving.

Abandon (www.google.com) is defined as, to cease to support or look after (someone); desert or give up completely (a course of action, a practice, or a way of thinking). In other words, LETTING GO, to discard or to relinquish! Most of the time I have witnessed people letting go before they have given themselves a chance to hold on. The root to abandonment could be associated and related to the term rejection, and often, rejection produces the idea of giving up on what one should be fighting for. This could lead to giving up on dreams, goals, aspirations, people, love and even life.

There is a famous TV series, entitled, *American Idol*, where individuals from across the country compete to become the next super star. They go into auditions with the hopes and the dreams of merely being good enough to get to the finals and be the overall winner. Their ultimate prize will be bragging rights and a recording contract. Not being a fan of the show since season 9, I just so happen to get a chance to watch an episode of a season in 2019. During the screening, I overheard an individual describe himself to the nations in a manner that to the casual listener, would just say, he is so humbled, but the analysts and the ones who believe that there is power in your words, may view it a little contrarily.

The young man had made it through the final additions and was shifted into the next round. Many who come to the auditions do not even get a chance to see or go to the next round. During this interview before performing in the round, he went from being excited about even getting through, to speaking down on himself before the next round even happened. His words were like this, "I know I may not be the best, and I am not the best singer here, but I'm going to give it my all." While the word "but" (a conjunction) cancels out the first part of the phrase, what I realize was that he was giving up on himself before he had the moment of competing. He was starting to abandon the possibility of what he was already accomplishing just because of what was happening around him. He had a case of what I call,-compare-itis (comparing himself), and intimidation. I would go as far as saying, Self-Rejection. I am not certain as to what the state of his outcome was, but I was moved by the lack of confidence that he exemplified in a place where he fought to get to. To me, he had already counted himself out. The fact that he would GIVE UP on himself before going into the fight, he was letting go before given himself a chance to hold on!

Listen, life will throw things your way that you may not be ready to catch. Circumstances will arise that you THINK you can't overcome. Even though these things happen and you're not sure of the outcome, or not sure of the process, doesn't mean you will not win. We must simplify the method of self-soothing! Convince ourselves that even though I do not know how it's going to happen, or how it's going to turn out, I must not give up on the possibility of what could potentially happen before I even start.

THE LARGER THE CUP

Growing up in an environment where there was a lot of drinking, warranted several things to possibly transpire in my life. One possibility was that I would walk away from all the gatherings knowing that having a drink wasn't for me, or the other possibility was that I would eventually allow that world to become a part of my world. The odds were always in front of me and the choice was ultimately mine.

I can recall one party around the age of 15 where I took my first alcoholic drink! I had just gotten in from bringing in the new year at church, and when I arrived home, there was a party going on. Cars parked on the grass, along the road side and people standing around laughing, talking, and shooting the breeze. The music was jumping in this little 2-bedroom house and of course the red cups were in hands. The beautiful part was my family were altogether in one place including cousins, uncles, and a few aunts but no one really in my age bracket. Due to this being a small little house on the prairie it was quite inevitable that I would be able to go in my room, close the door and not be distracted. So I figured well, while I'm here I might as well enjoy the festivities. I didn't plan to really enjoy all of them, but the cups and the way people were enjoying themselves called me to become like curious George. There is one cousin who shall remain nameless who poured me my first drink, not because they offered but because I asked. my cousin was reluctant at first for various reasons, one being I was way under age, two, If I got caught, they would get in trouble. They poured me a hefty cup of E & J with Coke! The first taste was not the best but as the night went on it got sweeter and sweeter, and my world literally was changing.

I paraded around the house with a red cup and was asked on several occasions what was in it by my nosey father, and each time I would say, "nothing but soda," very convincingly. Now the first few times my dad asked, I was cool, and I figured he would just leave me alone, but in typical parent fashion, when they are not convinced they will do their own investigation and police the situation at hand! That is exactly what my father did! He questioned me one more time and when I gave him my response, he grabbed the cup, put his hound dog nose inside and said, well, let's say a few choice words. By this time the party was coming to an end, my father pulled me into the room and asked me what was I doing and of course who gave me the drink? I had several options; I could tell the truth or I could work my way out of it! I could get someone in trouble or I could take it all by myself. Just as I was about to spill the beans, my intoxicated mother walked in and convinced my father that I picked up the WRONG CUP! There it was my liberation moment. That phrase, "he probably picked up the wrong cup" saved my life and my behind.

After everyone cleared the party, I laid down in a dark room with the assurance that I wasn't going to have to pay the price for a cup of drinking what I could not handle. I would have paid for it by getting a whipping from my father, but my body responded by giving me the worst headache and feeling of being on a roller-coaster I wasn't on at Busch Gardens. The room began to spin with my eyes closed, and I felt like everything I had consumed would be plastered all over the floor. I could recall yelling for my parents for some relief, and I was so thirsty! There was really nothing that my parents could do for me, I just had to ride this baby out and make today light, and thankfully I did, hungry and embarrassed by the result of over consumption.

Reflecting over this moment brought great joy, yet a revelation of not being able to handle a cup that was too much for me. Not just in size but what was in the cup. Often in life we think we can handle almost anything that comes in our life, but if we are honest, we can only handle things in stages. For example, I can handle things better now that I'm older, but at an immature age, some things consumed me. Just like that when cups of life and circumstance come our way, we must decide if we can handle them or not. It will save you time and energy. Think about if you would have not taken on so much in your life, that at this very point, this very moment, how much further you could be. So, what do we take away from reflecting on that moment? Take on what you KNOW you can handle, especially when it comes down to people and circumstances. Remember, handle the things you can and pray about the things you can't! You will find life to be a lot simpler that way. Drink only what you can and leave the rest for someone else.

THE CIRCUS

As a young boy I have always been fascinated with animals, and the big show. I could remember listening on the radio or watching commercial ads about the circus being in town. The clowns flashing on television, the elephants standing on two legs, and horses running around, all brought my curiosity to life and I wondered to myself what it would be like to see that show!

My father was the type of guy that whatever his son wants he will try his very best to make it happen. Well, in true Benjamin Stearns fashion, he did just that. One day out of the blue, I was headed to the circus! It was now my chance to finally go and see the lights, the clowns and to experience the joy of seeing exotic animals.

Upon our arrival, the rush of the noise and the excitement of trying to find our seats, to the kids running with popcorn and cotton candy bags in their hands literally set my pure soul on fire with anticipation of what was awaiting me. It was one of the best feelings in the world. As we settled in and the lights began to dim, and the announcer aroused, the intensity of the crowd grew like grape vines in the summer. The show begins and all you could see around you was the smiles on the faces of so many children and adults who were reliving a childhood dream. I could recall asking myself what would it be like to be a part of this great show and ride those beautiful horses, dance, and become an actor or entertainer in front of thousands of people? As time passed and I grew up, I often still ask myself what would it be like to be in and a part of the "greatest show on earth?" The only difference is I ask now from a different place.

From a child perspective, my asking was because it was so refreshing to see what I never saw, comprised of all the things I loved. But now from a different place I asked the question, how did they deal with the travel? Did the animals really like being handled? Did people die? Was it all that it appeared to be?

The circus was a great show and was very fun for individuals to indulge in but the circus wasn't for everyone to be a part of. After much observation over time, I realized that each individual and animal has a role to play to entertain millions of people. Their focus was to do just that "entertain." Each person must fit the part to make up the entertainment and sometimes it costs them their life! You see when you entertain, you go to great lengths to satisfy others versus yourself. You tend to do what is necessary to keep the focus on what is being presented and it is the intent of the entertainer or entertainment to leave individuals wanting more!

Being in the business of people, one can often find themselves in a place where they have associated with people who have dressed up, looked a part, have been put together with lights, camera, and action, but underneath all the glam there have been some things that were just like the circus - an act! Have you ever asked yourself, how did I get connected to the spectacle of a relationship, friendship, or circumstance? And after stepping back and looking at the ups, downs, highs and lows it brought you; you realize the only reason you stayed was because it was entertaining to a certain part of you?

I have found that when working with people and even pastoring individuals, some people delight in the foolishness of their lives and they want to draw people into the humdrum of their eventful, chaotic, and toxic world. Coming to grips with this, I begin to understand, everyone's personal issues or concerns are not mine. As harsh as that may seem, there has to be boundaries with some relationships. Looking back at some of these individuals and my experience of them, they were quite entertaining! Not necessarily from a comical or laughable place, but from a teachable learning residence. The behavior of enjoying a world of **chaos**. I have learned that I am more helpful from a distance, and would rather not take part of the foolery but rather be helpful from the outside. My view from the stands was better served, then being a part of the show.

You see, attending the circus versus being a part of it was more helpful. If I was really a part of the show, I would damage others as well as myself, and probably would have created a bigger circus within the circus. In other words, creating foolishness. Life will bring you experiences that we should learn from and most of the time we do not learn until we get there. I want to encourage you, let the show of other people's life teach you from a distance. You do not always have to be a part of something to know what's going on. A college friend of mine said it like this, "You never can tell what's going on in a circle until you are longer a part of the circle!" It is at those moments of not being apart that you realize how better off you are watching from a distance. Remember watching never hurt anybody, it is the biggest teacher of them all. If you ever hear, "ladies and gentlemen, boys and girls, children of all ages," coming from the aroma of a person in your life, be careful, for the show is about to begin, just make sure you are not participating.

YOU CAN

The book of Exodus, one of the books of Moses, is an explicit book that captures the bondage, the freedom, and the rebellion of a chosen people. It is a memoir of a voice of complaint to some and a lesson for many.

When going through this hardship experience, God hears the cry of his people and sends Moses to be the trailblazer to take on the task of rescuing his relatives from the traumatic relationship with the Egyptians. Upon them exiting Egypt, there were several accounts that God proves his care for them and would wisely guide them through his exit plan.

As the story moves forward, Pharaoh is reluctant on occasions and refuses to adhere to the request via Moses.

And the LORD spoke to Moses, "Go to Pharaoh and say to him, 'Thus says the LORD: "Let My people go, that they may serve Me. **Exodus 9:1**

Each time Pharaoh would deny the request, but even in his denial God always provided for the Israelites. He provided safety for them when he sent death to consume all the youngest of the babies, and even told them to ask the Egyptians what they would do before they left captivity. God always made sure that what he did for them was to not just prove his love for them but to affirm his commitment to his word. He remained consistent and even when it appeared that they would be left to die, he still displayed his faithfulness.

Upon their departure across dry land of the Red Sea, they would enter land that would become their holding place until the moment of progression happened for them to inherit the promised land. The place of quarantine for them was not a permanent place, but based upon their reluctance to honor, the short journey turned into what we know as the wilderness experience.

The purpose of God releasing them from the hands of the "enemy" was for their relationship to be reestablished. He wanted them to be free to get back to the place of worshiping him. But due to their bondage mentally their words of worship, became acts of complaints. They complained and they murmured, they murmured and complained so much that their lack of reverence turned into idol worship, which caused a major delay, and their level of gratitude was replaced with ungratefulness.

It is common to spend so much time on the issue at hand that we will forget about the process of where we have come from. Despite all that God had for all of them, some lacked the reverence that caused them to not make it to the promised land or the next phase of their life. You see, the Israelites spent so much wasted time on complaining, that they missed out on the fact that it was only temporary. In other words, they did not appear thankful that they survived.

Is this not the word that we told you in Egypt, saying, 'Let us alone that we may serve the Egyptians'? For it would have been better for us to serve the Egyptians than that we should die in the wilderness." Exodus 14:12

Being thankful must start from a place of one appreciating what is not anymore. Could it be that the Israelites were in a place uncertain of their future? Did wondering about their survival caused them to be unthankful in deliverance?   The result of them being in the wilderness for some did not end well, but for many a lesson learned. For those that learned the lesson they were granted to live in a land that flowed with milk and honey, and for some they were swallowed up in the ground.

So, I leave you with this question. Would it be better to complain about where you are and what you don't have, then to stay thankful-in a posture of gratitude until you reach the promise? Is it worth it to lose everything in complaining than to worship God for bringing you out?

Do yourself a favor and reflect on how much time you wasted complaining on what you don't have than the fact that you survived. I challenge you the next time you find yourself complaining about your life, think about

the person that is worse off than you. Replace your complaint with a
compliment to God for what he did not allow that you deserved and how much he thought of you to survive.

I WILL MAKE IT

TODAY, I confess with my mouth and believe **that I WILL MAKE IT!**

I will make it over_____!

I will make it through_____!

I will make it in_____!
Write your story of what you have MADE IT THROUGH to remind yourself!

LINED UP FOR YOU!
#FORWARDMARCH

Joshua who fought the battle of Jericho had nothing to worry about during his moment of conquering the city! In fact, everything that he needed was a setup for him to inherit the promise that was made, because things were lined up for him and the children of Israel.

The bible speaks of a promise that God made to his people and his servant Moses. He assured them that they would inherit the promised land, and it would be stocked with milk and honey! In other words, the place that was lined up for them would also be the place that would bless them. Now for this to happen, it did not mean the children of Israel would not have to do their part. They were commissioned to conquer but the requirement was obedience. The story goes on and clear instructions were given, all they had to do was follow and trust God in the process. They had a plan to conquer, and they did that. They spied, made friends to assist in the takeover, they marched, blew their instruments, shouted, and took over the city!

The purpose of this take over was not only because the lord promised them, but also because it was lined up for them. As you go throughout your day today, are there things that have been lined up for you to conquer? So, I ask, what is in your path to takeover that will set you up for the milk and honey? Your day was lined up for you! It was created and designed for you to be blessed! So, I encourage you to TAKE on the day and receive what God has lined up for you, it might just be the blessing you need to overtake you!

WHAT'S NEXT FOR YOU

TODAY! I am going to STAND WITH GOD! He Hasn't failed me yet, and He NEVER WILL! I decree and declare it!

Write what your next looks like!

My NEXT looks like....

WHO'S HOLDING UP YOUR ARMS

The book of Exodus is filled with wonder and excitement. This prolific book is a monument to the progression of overcoming and the movement to promise. The level of excitement that comes from this book speaks to the character and the heart of God; those readers would walk away impacted by the love of the father.

The love that God showed to his children not only speaks to his character, but to the willingness to make sure they were taken care of during their journey of being in the wilderness. Through Exodus God provided water, food, his rebuke, and his love. This was clearly a level of commitment and him holding up his end of the bargain to his covenant with them. During this journey, the children of Israel become unsure at times that the same God who brought them out of Egypt and across the Red Sea, would be the same God that would hold them up during what seemed like troubled times.

During one of God's moments with Moses their leader, the children of Israel would see yet again the promise of God. The children of Israel were not only at battle with themselves, but they often had to fight the armies that were of the valley. During a battle with the Amalekites, Moses stood from a far with his arms extended and hands lifted to ensure they would win the battle. Like some of us his arms got tired, and the word says, "that every time he would lower his arms, they noticed that they would lose the battle, and every time he would extend the arms, they would win the battle." One of the most important parts of this story is that there were two individuals standing, watching what was taking place, and upon their careful eye, they understood not only what was happening to their camp, but that they had the power to assist in the process. They begin to assist Moses by holding up his arms so that they might win the battle.

Today you may feel like you are losing the battle, that you are not going to win, but I want to encourage you that you are closer to winning than you think. How is that possible? Take a moment and look over your life and see first how far you have come. Then ask yourself who helped me? Once you find out who has helped you, ask yourself are they still here? If they are great, if not great. The season you are in is not determined by who is not there or who is there but determined by the hand of God and his plan for your life and sometimes that Plan is for people to help you along the way.

This was the case with Moses, even though he did a lot of work alone, he did not end alone. I will pose this question. Who are the Aarons and Hur's in your life? Are they willing to notice you, set you on a rock and lift your arms? Be reminded son/daughter, you are not in this alone, there are people around you who see where you are going, allow those people to HOLD UP YOUR ARMS!

BELIEVE HIM FOR YOURSELF

Seeing is believing is what most people would say who merely operate on their on-intuition versus FAITH. We all have done it, believe it or not. A time where someone told us something about someone or something and we may have said to ourselves, "I need to see that!" In some form or fashion, we ALL have needed to see it in order to believe it, and not based upon what others have said but for yourself.

Habitually in this walk I have found myself praying for others for their request about what they needed God to do on their behalf. How they needed God to work things out or stood in need of something major to happen for them that would lead them into another phase of their lives. As a person, it is not in my nature to not stand in another posture other than happiness, because of them receiving what they asked me to pray for alongside of them or even from others. In fact, I have ministered and been taught on rejoicing with others. One reason being is that, "if God could do it for them, surely he can do it for me!" And besides that, is what believers are supposed to do rejoice with those who rejoice. But have you ever stopped and asked yourself, when is it going to be my turn? Or, how is it that I can believe for everyone else and NOT believe God for what I am asking for?

Could it be that you have more faith in others than yourself? Or could it be that you do not want it that bad? In my experience with Christ, I have found that intercessory prayer is one of the best ways to get what you desire. Biblical content has shown that selfless acts reveal a great reward. Jesus being the ultimate sacrifice is probably the greatest example. Then you have the widow woman and her son that gave her last to the prophet and sacrificed what appeared to be their last and only meal. Finally, the temple ruler, who went to Jesus on behalf of his daughter who was fatally ill. All these accounts represented individuals whether related or not who wanted to believe God for others, and in turn those who were making the request known, also received the miracles.

HANG ON

As a Pastor, the leadership team and I often ask the question, why does it seem that people are not overcoming? And one of the counter questions I add to the question is, could it be that nobody is wanting to Testify?

The old church I grew up in use to have a portion of the service called Testimonial Service. This was not a separated service at a different time, but merely during the time of devotion., This was the time where the Deacons would get up and line a hymn (with no music), pray, and allow people to testify. I call it the first Praise & Worship method. This part of the service, individuals would sing another song and share their life experiences of overcoming or going through, through that song. Or some would get up and just thank the Lord for allowing them just to be in the building and others sometimes would tell how God healed them from certain things and just tell of the goodness of the lord.

These were some of the most POWERFUL moments in my life! It showed the boldness of people standing before their peers, how excited they were and how excited others were for them. But most importantly it showed the POWER of God and his MIGHTY hand still at work! You see it was the moment of testimony service where we heard how people were overcoming, and how the power of what God was doing in their life, could, would do the same in others. If he is the same God for the church of old, isn't he the same God of the church of now? If that is the case, why are we not sharing what God has and is doing in our lives.

Your overcoming isn't just about you! It is merely the reflection of who God is and what he has and is doing for you. Hiding testimonies is not the solution to helping people, it's the sharing that is most important. Why not share? Are you ashamed of what you have done? Or is it that you are still doing what you thought you overcame? I believe one of the reasons why we don't share as much is due to what people are going to think of what has happened. Think about how powerful you have become because of what you have survived in! How much smarter and wise you are! You see, your life is a testimony, the fact that you are alive is powerful. The fact that you survived the car accident, house fire, loved ones passing away, friends walking away is enough to share with someone that might be going through the same thing, but are waiting to hear from you!

Overcoming isn't just about you passing a trial but merely the fact that we have overcome due to the blood of the lamb and the word of our testimony. Based on this scripture it takes two things to overcome, the blood of Jesus and the sharing of our life experiences. Your words are meaningless without the blood, so they both go hand in hand. Your testimony is only powerful if you share it, hidden blessings can help anyone overcome. So, ask the question: who will overcome your story?

IT IS FINISHED

The final words from Jesus on the Cross, was *Tetelestai*. In Greek this word means, "to bring to an end, to complete, to accomplish." In our language today it would mean, IT IS FINISHED!

Some of the most powerful words, spoken by THE most powerful human being ever to walk this earth. He simply said to us that everything in the past and everything in the future is done! This simple meaning shares with us that, there is not anything new under the sun, but that, life is a fixed fight and we have already won! If that be the case, what is it in your life that you have not finished that needs to end?

Maybe it is past hurts, or present unforgiveness, maybe it is a chapter in your life that you need to move on from. Whatever that may be in your life, that needs to end today. Confess the words from our Savior, IT IS FINISHED. Today your nightmares come to an end, your past hurts come to an end. Your unforgiveness, heartaches, lack of motivation, whatever it is must come to an end. Start a new day by ending yesterday and decree over your life that it is finished.

ABOUT THE AUTHOR

Jermaine L. Stearns, is an ordained Elder, photographer, mentor and serves as a Pastor of Victorious Hope, located in Fayetteville, North Carolina and has been in ministry for over 15 years. He holds a Bachelor of Ministry from Andersonville Theological Seminary.

Stearns is the author of an inspirational cookbook entitled, *Food for Thought* and *Note to Self*. He is also a published songwriter and graphic designer. Originally a native of Columbia, South Carolina, He currently resides in North Carolina with his wife and three children.

www.ingramcontent.com/pod-product-compliance
Lightning Source LLC
Chambersburg PA
CBHW060342130626
46553CB00003B/1088